OPALESCING

MELISSA EATHERINGTON

Copyright ©2013 Melissa Eatherington

All rights reserved.

ISBN: 0615880673
ISBN-13: 978-0615880679

For R, for always believing in me, and for my children – if I can reach for my dreams, I know you will have even greater success with yours.

CONTENTS

Rowing	1
The Sea and Me	2
Opalescing	3
Magenta Midnight	4
The Blooming Edge	5
The Observers	6
Nothing Rhymes with Orange: a pantoum	7
Summer Night Haiku	9
Abandoning Time	10
Rolling Coins	11
Poet Valley	13
Setting	14
Minted Snow	15
Heart's Garden No. 6	16
On Writing	17
Mortal States	18
Silences	19
Gossamer Way	20
Sky Breach	21
Tobacco Barn Rain Shelter	22
Enraptured	23
New Designs	24
Ghostbane Sunrise	25
Purple Monday	26
Existence	27
Truth in the Broken Mirror	28
Hidden Song: an alba	29
Shadow Tunnel	30
Nightmare	31
Astronversation	32
To Ben Johnson and His Admirers: an elegy	33
Laughing at the Rain	34

Druid's Pledge	35
Sweeping: a villanelle	36
Knowing	37
Crosswords	38
Green Blue Gray	39
Glass Squares	41
Leftover Laughter	42
Violins	43
Gone Walkabout	44
Exquisite	45
Muddy	46
Passing	47
Rain Pantoum	48
The Coming Drum	49
Curtains	51
My Grand Estate	52
Blood and Honey	53
Southern Meteorology	54
Crown of Reluctance: a sestina	55
Spindle Fields	57
Brick Butterflies	58
Dawn in the Country	59
October Travels	60
Shrinking	61
Eden	62
Faithless	63
Starflight	64
Another Parting	65
Jacks	66
Afternoon Stroll	67
The Other Grail	68

Rowing

As into troubled sleep I fall
I answer to the beck and call
Of restless dreams, storms that blow
Their sandman mists to and fro.
In the illuminating darkness, now I see
The illusion of truth revealed to me
By everything that came before
And everything that is no more
The promise of things yet to be
No longer chained to reality
A waking dream, a dreaming wake
With every breath the dreamer takes
Time flows at the mercy of the id
There where deepest desires are hid
And inner wishes slumber deep
As I lie there, fast asleep.

The Sea and Me

The sea and me –
we dance. We dance and push and pull and churn
and deepen.

And I –
I am Atlantis, storied, mythic
a drowned city
thriving
as the flame beneath the water,
primal,
a sand-freckled soul alight.

Opalescing

I have felt the nagging tattered edges
Of my own shattered doubts
Chewing on the corners of ragged shards in shadows
As unshakeable as spring's inimitable, tenacious
    splendor
Dancing on the edge of unwieldy, laughing dawn.
I am only mortal; I cannot hide the sun
And thus it explodes into my heart again
Glittering diamond demons pulsing quickly
Ahh, magnificence
Opalescent glory backlit in shimmering flames
And so I return.

Magenta Midnight

In the grass that grows glass flowers
There's a place where time stands still
And crystal stars betray no hours
Between sweet breaths of ragged will.

Fear not the shadows that loom in moonlight
They will retreat at break of day
Swords cannot abide a magenta midnight
And no blood spills in terror's sway.

I pluck a rose that has no thorn
And place it – and me – in your tormented hands
Fragile, trusting, we await the morn
And a ship to bear us from these lands.

The Blooming Edge

Standing on the cusp of morning
With the first breath of day shimmering before my
    eyes
I find myself on a cliff, a thousand flowers below
Sparkling as they shake night-mist from tender petals.
I marvel at their freedom, at the very peace that
    eludes me.
They slept through the night, bowed heads of
    shadowless thoughts
And upon waking, were redeemed with the first rays
    of dawn.
That could be me, I think, and I burst into bloom.

The Observers

The last snowflake of winter falls before me
And the world of my waking falls silent.
Blanketed in truth, the night hurls back my reflection
From a thousand pairs of watchful eyes.

Nothing Rhymes with Orange: a pantoum

Nothing rhymes with orange, even anger.
That's the very last cold-drenched lie
for the right-handed robber and the southpaw forsaken.
I'm sorry I let you betray me.

That's the very last cold-drenched lie;
The thunder god has me in his white-hot grip.
I'm sorry I let you betray me,
a sacrifice upon the altar of rain.

The thunder god has me in his white-hot grip.
Frozen tears glitter in their lonely tracks,
a sacrifice upon the altar of rain,
and the waters run hissing into steam.

Frozen tears glitter in their lonely tracks,
seeking the light of one who lingers,
and the waters run hissing into steam.
Rivulets slink in silence, drop by drop,

seeking the light of one who lingers
as penance falls upon the prisoner waiting.
Rivulets slink in silence, drop by drop
down the shrine of fear now crumbling.

As penance falls upon the prisoner waiting,
a slender finger traces a path of dust
down the shrine of fear now crumbling
and sweat replaces weeping.

A slender finger traces a path of dust.
There is only one road to redemption
and sweat replaces weeping
in this trial by fire.

There is only one road to redemption
For the right-handed robber and the southpaw
forsaken.
In this trial by fire
nothing rhymes with orange, even anger.

Summer Night Haiku

Crickets chirp at dusk
Train whistles in the distance
Fans slowly whirl 'round.

Abandoning Time

Leave me, Father Time
Let life drift by, slow and sweet
Give me ample verse and endless rhyme
An angel's soul to greet.

Do not rush to take away
The simple joys I find in now
Instead, let me live day by day
No wrinkles hurried to my brow.

Allow me these moments and I'll cherish as gold
Precious times remembered when
A fourth score of autumns I shall behold
These are the years love lives again.

Father Time, now while I am young
And steady hand holds flowing pen
Hasten not bright words' bow unstrung
And I shall be blessed to call you friend.

Rolling Coins

Ah, Indiana
Crossroads and cornfields and skies that stretch
    forever
Missouri, California, and the Old Line State.

Clink,
clink
My little ones need new shoes
and a dirty eagle spreads his wings beneath my
    thumb.

North Carolina and Ohio
Dulled silver battle lines with aviation between
A schoolchild's headache and little more.

I wonder, too
What these coins – so many Lincolns –
Have bought with their stoic faces and smudged
    fronts:

A loaf of bread? Gum and smokes?
A six pack before the big game?
The test that revealed new life in the making?

I'll never know.
Money talks, but says very little
Staccato notes colliding, tangling on the floor.

Georgia, and the summer sun warms my neck at
    midnight.
Virginia, Tennessee, Wisconsin, Maine
Year after year and memories fade.

Bright copper glints from beneath a dark nickel

This year, so full of promise
And last year, already heavy and gray.

Thin dimes hide in the shrinking pile
   – one so mangled it must have run under a car;
I pick it up and toss it aside. Guilt, ten cents.

The cosmos heaved up a knotted timeline on my
     carpet.
1964 – 1982 – me.

The American Dream, sung and scraped from counter,
     desk, and glove boxes
From floor and parking lot and "Have a nice day" thrus
Resonating through bridges and wheat fields and
     silver Liberty
Thick paper throats full of metal.

Poet Valley

Down in the valley
Of the fog-shrouded mountains
I wandered lonely as Wordsworth's cloud
As if the valley had called me out
While the rest of the world lay sleeping

The face of time boldly returns my searching gaze
Gentle mockery as yet benign
Will not remain forever so, but
Somehow, even this,
The touch of something I do not yet know
Brings comfort to a restless heart.

Setting

Dawn
Early, bright
Rising, waking, warming
Sunrise, roosters, moon, stars
Darkening, twinkling, cooling
Sunset, peaceful
Dusk.

Minted Snow

I have not yet written today into my own existence
Watching the snow fall in silence, serenity
As pure as fresh mint on my tongue, sweet and deep.
I wish to leave this day untouched in memory
Alive in beauty, undiluted across the years –
If only peace fell as generously, as quietly
As effortlessly as winter mountain snow.

Heart's Garden No. 6

Does it stand to reason,
If poets ran out of rhyme
Love would last but for a season
Instead of transcending time?
Happiness would wither away
Heartache would grow in its place
Forget-me-nots lost in the pouring rain
Empty arms in a false embrace
Sowing truth and reaping lies
Watered by ever more tears
The hope that bloomed slowly dies
In the fading light more gloom than cheer.

On Writing

I hate waiting.
But then, you do not hear it
For you, the solitude is perfect, quiet
But not so for me.
I hear a poem coming
Feel the rhythm of unwritten lines humming in my
      fingers,
And I wait for them. It's all I can do.
The anticipation, the burning hunger of pen!
That furious attraction to the blank sheet of paper!
This yearning to touch creativity unborn!
I wait...and wait...and then,
Like birds up from a bush when you least expect them
Erupting a hundredfold in singular sweetness
Beauty in rapt rainflight, pure
The words come at last.
Wistfulness granted, in majesty they come
Splendiferous words
They come!
Oh, sweet, beautiful enchantress Muse!
Hold me in your spell a moment longer
As my aching fingers forget their growing torment
And I write.

Mortal States

I may die in Kansas on a cloudy day
Last time was in the rain;
I just couldn't help it and I fell away from myself.
As anyone could tell you who's ridden the plains
Tasted the freedom of irrationality and bittersweet
    grasses
Growing wild and abandoned out of the thankless
    ground
It's easy to do – to fall, to forget.
How was I to know I couldn't fly?
After all, if dreams take wing
Why
can't
I?

Again the end comes before a real beginning
And I rediscover truth, or it me.

Damn truth.
This time I live for lies
And if imagination does me in
Then at least I can say I died living
Not poisoned by the brackish waters of a stagnant,
    unstirred heart
And that's something, even in Kansas.

Silences

What have I to do but listen?
How dare your silence speak to me,
Betraying all you never say?
A cold wind under distant stars
Soliloquy of a muted heart

Would you break me with a smile
Or kill me with a tear?
Will you shatter the chains holding me here
Just to watch me fall so far?
Forgive me if I've forgotten who you are.

Gossamer Way

Aimless footsteps wandering along a path at sunset
I pass by places of utter green
Overwritten with glistening gossamer threads.
An earth-grown tapestry achieves humble glory
In the ebbing light of a forgotten place.

Sky Breach

Breach of sky
Blur of light-swept clouds' confusion
Blue scar across gray relief
Thoughts scattering on fickle wind
Heart's reflection back from heaven's gate
Softening in the falling shades of night
Darker, deeper now
See not with eyes alone
Lest you do not see me at all.
All is revealed and all is hidden
In the same moment
By the same movement.
Embrace the future or let it go
And grieve not for sweet inconstancy
Elusive now as the morning sun.

Tobacco Barn Rain Shelter

Wordward
Wind sword
Silence into shadow shards
Opening crack
Don't look back
Fleeing from a sky turned black
Frightened, young
Bottom rung
Leaves of gold from ceiling hung
August heat
Driving beat
Tin roof drum of unseen feet
Splish splash
Thund'rous crash
Dust to dust and ash to ash
Windswept
Promise kept
Barren land but not bereft
Fade away
Out to play
Sun yet shines on cloudy day.

Enraptured

I will be more than I seem
As long as that's not OK
You'll still be trapped within your dreams
When first light fails at break of day
And mortals cry out for their God
Long-dead faith breathes new life in them
And angels grace poor rage-riven sod
In a place at once free and condemned.

New Designs

Sharp roofline startled me deeply today
Cutting into endless blue
Honed edge where brick met vast open sky
Where what *is* contrasted with what doesn't have to
 be
Hardened realities and unformed dreams alike in
 beauty
As I shook myself and continued on my way.

Unfinished, I stand waiting
For some unspoken command that will not come
Save through my own voiceless desire
And then the sky is mine,
The buildings
Mine to crumble, mine to shield
Mine to redesign.

Ghostbane Sunrise

Mirror reflecting lack of light
In a crowded but empty room
A restless drifter in a house not right
With walls that drip, streaked with gloom.

Down the hall, close the door
Lonely hands cover weary face
Stale tears now hidden as before
But never again in this place.

Knowing too much but never enough
To ever fully comprehend
The lure of deceiving waters rough
Everyone else is drowning in

The past is a cruel executioner
Hope and the future its favorite prey
But one let go; it cannot hold her
And here is where she will not stay.

There is a dam soon to break, she knows
There are the damned; they will break too
Wading through fragile shells and shadows
The drifter reaches freedom and hard-bright truth.

Purple Monday

There is a place
Where Time runs screaming from the shadows that
 dog its steps
Where moonlight wanders down sour black paths
And even your tears are broken

The hounds of hell chase madness from a purple
 Monday
And seven times seven
A tattered, trampled princess stares up from the
 sodden ground
Awaiting the white horse she knows will never come.

Long-pressed flowers bleed from musty-faced books
Staining the hours of forgotten days –
Dawn will not linger here
Wake quickly, or risk entombment within a dream.

Existence

I am the fires of frosty late fall,
the blazing over-stoked hearth,
the ancient warmth of coming home.
I am the flame-leafed trees,
shaking out browning banners
in the hint-of-winter breeze.
I am autumn's daughter,
Brighid's handmaid, kissed by thunder,
braiding dreams of earth, storm, and sky.

Truth in the Broken Mirror

Life stares out at me, returning my intense gaze
At once tempting as it threatens
As I search for answers to questions I haven't asked –
Do I even really want to know?
Yes – and something precious shatters.
A new mystery unfolds before me,
How since none of it matters, everything does
And if love is good, and good and evil balance
Then evil exists because we love –
But I thought money was evil's demon root
And I'd love him anyway.
Reality, time – all subjective
But you can't go back to yesterday.
And the me that *is* smiles
At the me who somehow used to but could never be,
A rueful grin amongst slivers on the floor
And the only price I pay
Seven years' bad luck.

Hidden Song: an alba

Night drops notes of quiet perfection
Music composed in crystal starlight shining
Lips, arms dance at heart's direction
Silver moon over glad-broken long pining

Sweet kiss of dusk on ripe fruit lingers
Swaying gently in wanton breeze
Just in reach of thirsting fingers
Yearning limbs trembling to please

Burn the hours in the night
Go down in flames, love's bright light
Get up, get up all too soon
Bid farewell to the fading moon

Songs of passion with dawn interred
No wrath of daylight dark incurred.

Shadow Tunnel

Tunnel of shadows and trees of dust
Branches latticed between footprints and sky
Lace curtains belie black shutters
And the malevolence of spiked bushes, empty porch
Ill-hidden by the white picket fence.
All is silent in the bold gray stillness
And I would not walk in those shadows
Only to become a reflection of someone I never knew
Trapped behind sun-glared glass.

Nightmare

Shadows of a dream
Echoes of unspeakable evil
Haunt my waking moments
And chilling images scream through my mind.
I shake myself to clear away
The menacing darkness's whispered memory
Banish it from me now! I cry
But it clings

The wind, no longer friendly, blows
Through my heart as if it knows
The malice that stalked my night

And I wish it would rain.

Astronversation

Answer me now, ye stars I call
Arrest for a moment your celestial fall
You cannot possess the purest power
Your centuries of life but a fleeting hour
You know nothing of beauty, nor joy
If aught but love your schemes employ
And so, without care pass me by
Flee from your cloak of midnight sky
Back into the emptiness from whence ye came
Heaven's glory has a brighter flame
That which by the smallest spark
Rescues souls from the deepest dark
And resides within an angel's heart
And for him, always in mine.

To Ben Johnson and His Admirers: an elegy

Curse that Ben Johnson, ungrateful beast
Given seven years – six months the least
Never will I hear my child's tiny cry
Or lift my voice in sweet lullaby.

And yet you wonder why I still grieve
Having less to lose, ten weeks conceived?
More, say I, I lost than thee!
Thou who sat thy son upon thy knee
You held your daughter, safe and warm
I rock cold womb and empty arms.

But love is strong and will not falter
The hand of mercy will grace faith's altar
And barren forever I'll not remain
All that is lost will in joy be regained.

Laughing at the Rain

Earlier, I laughed at the rain
Splattering on my mortarboard
But not touching my soul with its sorrow.
Later, the silent puddles in the dark
    – Each an ocean of sadness –
Could not match my own
As we spent our last moments together.

Who could have known, when this journey began
That we'd end up saying goodbye in the Wal-Mart
    parking lot?

Somehow I always imagined it
So different from the way it was
I thought I would be strong enough
To walk away sans tears, sans you –
As it was, I could barely even stand.
And I think my heart was breaking
It hurt so much to know things could never be the
    same.
I wished I could go back to the naïve happiness
Of laughing at the rain.

Druid's Pledge

I pledge allegiance to the quest for peace
And to all life, for which it stands.
One world, indivisible under heaven
With hope and harmony for all.

Sweeping: a villanelle

You from my heart I cannot sweep
Nor bar from my dreams your sweet-voiced call
Or learn the secrets that you keep.

The night finds me restless in my sleep
Among twisted sheets, a truth unmauled:
You from my heart I cannot sweep.

I would not make the flowers weep
Or shatter friendship's silent hall
But to learn the secrets that you keep.

While passions lurk within the deep
I wonder if I should tell at all
Since you from my heart I will not sweep.

As time steadily over all doth creep
I would decipher your soul's rise and fall
To learn the secrets that you keep.

Strangers no more, the price too steep
I am torn by leaving, incomplete – recall
You from my heart I can never sweep
Nor learn the secrets that you keep.

Knowing

A tiny chipmunk stops, methinks
(And turns on me those piercing eyes)
To peruse my soul and never blinks
Then scurries elsewhere in surprise.

A strange man stares as if he knows
The answer to where my shadow goes
(With luminescent, hostile eyes)
And far away, a raven cries.

Crosswords

I wonder if she ever cries
In the small house full of light
For the sunshine is cold there, and cruel
Illuminating the old forgotten colors
And filling the hollows with silence
Where laughter used to reign.
They blow through like the wind these days
Sometimes unexpected, and never for long
And then are gone again, and their voices fade
Into younger nights and photographs
Crowding corners and staring out,
No challenge to loneliness now or ever.
The old woman's faded beauty
Sighs from a window, outside now
As she settles into her worn recliner
The local paper in her wrinkled hands
The daily crossword her true companion.
I wonder if she cries.

Green Blue Gray

The ocean waters of our friendship murmur a faint wind
    song
Benign, waiting, unfathomable
Salt spray gently stinging my heart
Leaving it glittering like the midnight diamond you are.

The scent of roses, the bittersweet candied pink of petals –
They have no place here and refuse to grace my tongue
As I seek soul-bladed words to sway you from complacency
Firestarter, I am.

Your name springs from my lips unbidden, the green-blue-
    gray of it braided like ribbons
There ain't a body on this earth for whom the sound is
    sharper
Cutting into my thoughts even as I write
Deepening the canyon in my sunset soul
With that magnetically piercing gaze.
Stonecutter steady, tropical eyes meet autumn's echoes
Throwing impossible sparks that once would have had me
    flinching
But for that every now and then, when I catch a glimpse
A quickly flashed reflection of myself holding the moon
An illusion, or real? But I thought you were master of our
    ebb and flow
So I'll compromise between thought and reality
And I'll conjure the moon betwixt us both.

Gentle silver light splashes down behind my eyes
You see it also, I hope and I fear
And the sweet-scalded ocean rolls violently, trembling,
    uncertain
On the brink of consuming itself or the world.

She likes you, that Red, that redheaded girl
Under Blue Ridge skies, the cold mountain rain
Splatters truth into the growing tsunami.

You will soon have to safeguard the moon
You must; you shall be the sentinel of skies
And you will quell the imbalance raging.
That electrifying, immortal gaze stuns the earth to silence.

New-muted fires skitter across the calming waters
Riding the last waves before dying in the night
Lingering forever as smoky ghosts.

You wish the ocean not to stir
Thus it is so, because it must be.

Perhaps on your rounds in the blue, blue sky
You'll notice the canyon, parched in the winter sun
And when the moon rises again in your precious care
Fragile silver beams catching the light of your soul,
Echoes of another light shall shimmer from the darkness
Weaving into your own,
Dipping down into shadows and out again
As we may have done by then.

When that moment unveils the deepest truth
The ocean may joyfully abandon its bounds
Flooding the chasm long-ago forged
And frozen, waiting for beautiful, at last heralded
When dawn's first light comes.

And perhaps we shall stand on the same side of the newly
        christened river,
I, the earth-guardian of my heart
And you, keeper of the moon I once held:
Friendship double-forged by time and water
Now shining with the promise of rough-hewn gems
Miles and forever deep.

Glass Squares

Winter wind-blown chaotic gentleness
Falling just so, whiteness caught and released again
Sped up, upward dance, falling fast and cold and light
Wait, switch, release – time in for dreams and snow
Going anywhere and nowhere all at once
Striaght-fall to push the distant trees into a painting
Nearer branches bare, pleasing in their brownness
     now
Alter reality one flake at a time
And I will dance with you from an upstairs window
One fragile moment, beauty everlasting.

Leftover Laughter

Leftover laughter, both felt and seen
Rustles through joyful trees
Happiness decked out in green
Colored glee on autumn breeze

A single strand of spider's web
Trailing through the air
Fragile touch, life's flow and ebb
Ethereal dreams haunting there.

Violins

Willingly adrift on a deep purple ocean
Violent violet waves flowing rich as melted metal
    through the air
Mounting tension, sweet release suspended
Rising from velvet to silk and back again
A silver flash, a swirling turn
Again that coppered illusion
A few bronze, glittering notes left where they would
    spill
Into this symphonic sea.

Gone Walkabout

Gray, tree-lined highway
Overhead clouds are unconfining
Not a wall, but a gate of fluff
To freedom.
Speed trap
Nyah, can't catch this!
I sail by untouched,
Unhurried on my happy, rambling way.
Late afternoon sunlight
Glints through ecstatic branches.
For once, all lights say go,
No hint of red to hinder me
Along this old stretch of road
And I wonder if anyone else can feel
The sheer joy coursing through me
As they whiz by on the other side.
Blue, white, green and gray
Seem to me the perfect patchwork
Of a world reborn under the hum of my wheels
Awaiting the first spoken word.

Exquisite

Exquisite
Your breath as you stand there, aloof from life
Waiting for daybreak with your firm hands raised
As if in quiet supplication
Or bold contemplation of this, Nature's finest hour
The mirror image of the unbroken soul
Captured in dewdrops newly set aflame
In the untainted congregation of grass
As the grayness that hushes the most strident hum
Gives way, unchanged but yielding to the dawn.
Are you God, raising the sun with a silent command?
Or are you mortal, awaiting your fate with quiet dignity
As you challenge the sky to take from you what could never be lost?
No matter.
Here, now, in this place
You are.
And in this are-ness, you exist as nothing else
And so are beautiful.

Muddy

Rain-made red mud,
Why do you hold my gaze
Like the stubborn boot my foot gave up just now?
Was that not a fit enough offering
To such a treacherous, greedy place?
Is it not enough you slow my stride
But you must keep my eyes downcast too?
No, you do not hold such fascination for me
Your sucking ugliness a sienna stain
On the precious hours in this day.
Sun-kissed and made to exist no more
So you and I will be tomorrow.

Passing

i didn't know
you couldn't say
and so we passed
and the years fell like autumn leaves
through realms where kings still laugh and play

where blue and blissful music drifts
notes flaring into midnight flowers –
so many blooms per heart.

Rain Pantoum

As the rain falls in rhythm
– The beat of nature's song
The wind howls a haunting tune
The storm lasts all night long

The beat of nature's song
Lightning dances through the clouds
The storm lasts all night long
As thunder claps its approval.

Lightning dances through the clouds
A dazzling performance so high
As thunder claps its approval
Black enfolds the midnight sky.

A dazzling performance so high
The wind howls a haunting tune
Black enfolds the midnight sky
As the rain falls in rhythm.

The Coming Drum

"Come," I said
And "Come," he said
(Come, come, come)
But you did not come.

With earth and air and fire and song
Through mountain days I beat my drum
Come, come, come

And when at last you'd come to me
I heard the rhythm of our lives
Drumming, drumming, drumming

Into your blood I poured my song
Drum, come, come
So long I waited for your coming
(Come, come, come)
Again you did not come.

With life and breath and fire and song
Again I bade you come
Again I beat my drum
And suddenly you were coming

Too fast you were to meet your life
And Death heard his icy dance
Coming, coming, coming

Into your blood I poured my song
Drum, come, come
Into my blood hands reached the wrong
And I was drumming, drumming, drumming

'Twixt life and death you heard my song
Drumming, drumming, coming
Death slipped away; with you I cried
Come, drum, come

Learn this lesson well, my son
(Drumming, drumming, drumming)
Hold fast to life four scores or more
And when Death again knocks at your door
Tell him you're not coming.

Curtains

Sadness deeper than the tears that cannot fall
Dark-drenched silent river that finds no fountain
Eleventh hour betrayal of all
Haunting pain older than man or mountain
The promise of a sapphire sky's heartstorm happiness
Broke with the diamond stars at dawn
The one who came with nothing leaves with less
Across this final act the curtain is drawn
She had only one wish, as her soul lay crying
One last chance to meet an old friend
But love, like life, left her dying
No one forever evades the end.

My Grand Estate

Empty paper, silent pen
Inspiration alone again
Just out of expression's farthest reach
That despised chasm not often breached

I wish to dream legend to life
To carve reality with a bard's bright knfe
And with breath of soul shake dust off mind
That all who read my words might find
Some message in these bits of me
The poet's eternal legacy.

Blood and Honey

I hold your bright words close 'til morning
    –   the only button holding closed
my patched soul-jacket against the chill of winter
dreams.

"I love you" flows from cracked lips,
sweeter than blood. The honeyed moonlight pauses,
holding its own against impatient dawn.

Southern Meteorology

Blow and rage in your transient fury
Free the wrath of a thousand possessed Poseidons over
      land and over sea
But do not rob anyone of home;
Even the poorest man would mourn his cardboard castle.

Go ahead; snap burly branches like cheap plastic toys
Rip down power lines, leaving them writhing raggedly on
      cold wet streets
Or coiled like haphazard snakes exiting Eden
But only if the hospitals have generators that work.

I was born near the coast; I grew up with your kin
Where you are as common in summer as fireflies
And I have seen you before.

I remember your sister, who jumped over land
She was violent; she tried to kill me
But the tree fell the other way, into a car
Instead of through the room where I watched,
Trembling and fascinated.

I remember your brother, too, who screamed rain for days
Mild-mattered, but wet and lingering
He brought the underground stream up
   – and the pasture land down –
Until they met in startled new gulches of rushing muddy
      water.
The horses were *not* amused.

You are nothing new to me
Spend your windy soaking tantrum and begone.
And when you have passed, we will trickle from
      leaf-spattered doors,
Squinting in the sudden sunlight
The young and the elderly
Playing a grown-up game of pick up sticks.

Crown of Reluctance: a sestina

Clouds of meaningless conversation blur and run
Like cheap watercolors through my effervescing mind, and as
 if a king
Were me, or I him, I stride straight through the crowd, above
 the cobalt sky
And below my own thoughts. As I slip away from mundane
 and toward you,
My reign strengthens, conquering a thousand steadfast hearts
 in a realm of pulsing blue
As I outrace all but the fastest falling night.

Overripe, I have waited too long, and this will be my night
In shining *amor*; our soul-waters shall wake and run
Through long-parched riverbeds once drowned in sorrow's
 children. This brand new blue
Fades quietly into white crystal, and I stand upon Earth's
 frosty crown, a soft-haired girl king
With eyes of fire and spirit to match. It is with honor but not
 in glory that you
Have come to me, to offer the rough-cut truth instead of
 golden lies under an implacable sky.

Your words are simple, shaped with the working man's life,
 but those in the sky
Care little for such things. I am not one of them, you know; I
 do not fear the night
Or what the darkness brings. Bat wings are as beautiful to me
 as the flight of doves, and you
In all your wisdom say such things are meant to be. If I have
 run
From my past, from myself, you care not, and I say you are a
 king
Among kings, though no royalty you possess. My true blue

Friend, my late-night confidant, you alone understand my blue
Commoner's heart. I never asked for elevation; I despise with
 a passion the sky
Throne to which I am bound. Oh, would that you were my
 king

Beloved, my king among the stars! At least on this one
    fleeting night,
In this precious string of moments my heart will later caress
    as rosary beads, I run
From no man. We breathe the same jasmine-scented air, and
    you

Lay one hard-worked hand on my pristine shoulder, evoking a
    warm smile. I wonder if you
Know that you are my fount of redemption. Your steady blue
Thoughts pierce the angst in my soul, and I feel the jagged
    edges of my being run
Smooth in the company of my kindred spirit. Such a divisive
    sky,
That the sun and moon may never shine at once! This night
Seems like the first night, so many eons ago, when perhaps
    the first king

Sat with his trusted counselor and searched for the brightest
    star, a shining answer. I may be the last king
To ever walk these enchanted hills, and if I failed in honesty,
    if I lied to you,
I would be unworthy before even the ancient, mighty oaks
    keeping silent watch all through the night.
They reign for the time deemed their own, crowned in green
    below the impassive blue
Banner overhead. So I will gather my courage, draw strength
    from the sky
And from the hushed stillness of the ground, and I will rise
    even as my blood does run

From cold to fire, running through my heart with a hammering
    ferocity befitting a king
As I bare my soul, wondering at the touch of my pale hand
    upon your well tanned face. The sky is deaf but never
        are you
So open to hear me as in this steel-split moment set down as
    blue on our wordless, perfect night.

Spindle Fields

Final hours turn and dwindle
Moon hangs caught on a blood-red spindle
Footsteps falter in fallow fields.

Night-deep silences unending
A bright-dark summons souls are wending
Crimson balance, rend and heal.

Dream and dare not breathe too deep
Nor mourn lost lifetimes spent asleep
Lone rusted bell, stirring, peals.

Brick Butterflies

Conditioned for casualties, we are not and never could be
It is false nature, blasphemer! I can see your world:
Soaring brick and mortar butterflies
Exploding rainbows across a cloudless sky
Behold the creations of a modern war-god
Flowers falling under the fallible wheels of a hateful chariot
Winging fancy flight's last humming breath
One dying note at a time
A patriotic requiem, a song well-bled
For the children of the earth.

Dawn in the Country

The night
like my hardened heart
seems impenetrable
a black fortress
silent
intimidating
but slowly
it gives way
reluctantly surrendering
to the gray dawn, and
the mist
rises from the ground
lingering in the morning air
like a haunting melody.

October Travels

As the leaves start turning colors again
And a familiar chill settles in the air
Proliferating pumpkins herald the coming of another
    fall
And Jack Frost rolls out his welcome in fragile,
    glittering splendor.
The scent of burning wood greets me like an old friend
I journey forward but my mind drifts back in time
To other autumns in other places
And people who scattered through the years
Leaves on the winds of change
Memories cling to every sight and sound surrounding
    this season
Some as vivid as the sunset in all its hasty autumn
    glory
Others ethereal wisps that whisper, "Remember...
Remember...."
...and then fade on the crisp night air
Leaving me to reminisce alone
As I travel on.

Shrinking

I remember when you were only broken
Not shattered or damaged far beyond repair
That was before you met *him*
The man with all the answers
(and none of them)
But he had a free-flowing pen and a fresh prescription pad
Itchy fingers and smooth words
And the very latest in mental chains.
He told you your problems were all in your head
And that was enough
Down you went, and now they are
And yet you still come back for more
Like a tattered moth to a twisted flame,
Your dependency a sick parody of a normal life
Living from dose to dose
Instead of day to day
Until you couldn't find your way back if you tried.
And you still go through the motions
But your laughter, like your hope
Rings hollow in your heart.
You don't know how or when it began
Because you are never really there.
Life has become shadows
And you, a fragile shell afraid of the sun
Fragmented and scattered in a dozen different bottles.
Though they are small, your captors are strong
(only because you believe them so)
You seek salvation in your hell
Your demons are your heroes
And him above them all.
He paints your reality with brushstrokes of pills
An ever-changing kaleidoscope of confusion
And you stumble through time
Toward any kind of oblivion that passes for release –
But there is no escape
From your bottled existence.

I remember when you were only broken...

Eden

When that hazel heaven unlocked meets
Eyes of earth,
Amber vibrance hidden deep and richly sown,
Like gladly melting glaciers, all walls sublime
Down, gone, and in their place
Fire
Leaping flames of joy and desire
And there is nothing else again.
In that nothing, you are everything
Molten passion rolling forth
Devouring mountains and valleys of hot, writhing flesh
In an all-consuming wave.
Earth and sky tremble together,
Interlocked in ecstasy,
The world reforged in minutes
From the ashes of original sin.

Faithless

I am tuning out, but slowly
Like the well-timed creak of an unseen closing door.
Today I will make no offering
The buzz and click of worship will not assault my ears
And the dual three-pronged altars sit empty on the
      walls.
I need nothing from Progress today,
Nothing at all, just my own quiet thoughts.
Escape with me to yesterday
To the solitude of self, of time, of wonder.
Rejoice with me under an old, broad oak
For blue sky, pristine paper, willing pen
And cry with me
When the mockingbird sings a ringtone Mozart.

Starflight

She turned to kiss the weeping soul
Of a willow, long forgotten.
And as the water spilled from her destiny
It grew, spring ice begotten.
The umber clouds bequeathed a throne
And hurled it down with thunder,
And as she stood there, open-mouthed,
The stars took flight in wonder.

Another Parting

Tell me where you go at night,
The dreams you keep inside.
The chill of autumn creeps into my soul.

While the world sleeps alone
I find a crowd inside my head.
Where are you? So many thoughts, such a long pause.

I shiver when I think of leaving this place.
All my memories, the happiness I choose to keep -
Everything came from here.

Will you leave then forever,
Dusty footprints in my heart never to be renewed,
Or will you save the fateful day for me, a hero among thoughts?

Oh, please don't banish me from your heart.
Mine grows colder at the very thought
And I will not go quietly if you send me.

You are one of the few I trust
Don't break it, please; I tremble with fear
But after reflection, I think I know enough to smile.

I believe you will stay
And the air becomes still with sleep
An easier breath to breathe at last.

Jacks

Putrescent pumpkins
Sunken mouths and vacant eyes
October, *adieu*.

Afternoon Stroll

Arriving again amidst ponderous green
Surrounded by effervescing colors
I walk in water from a giant's leaky dream-shroud
Droplets dancing through a poet's painted landscape
Crepe myrtles drape overladen branches
Sagging under the weight of ten thousand dripping
    blooms
Glistening pink beauty bowed to kiss the marigolds
Sweeping the sodden earth's fresh-washed green
    carpet
Rainy-day Nature's caress
Enfolding my Muse like shining wet ivy on oaks.

The Other Grail

I will taste the fruit of dusk
Fresh ripened light-longing
Warm, golden words
Glinting off the hands that hold the shimmering cup
Moonlight's silver non-darkness gleaming
Brimming, yet still against the lip of the chalice
The promise of sleep and a hint of dreams.

ABOUT THE AUTHOR

Melissa Eatherington was born and raised in eastern North Carolina. She traded proximity to the beach for the stunning Blue Ridge Mountains, receiving her B.A. in English from Western Carolina University in 2005. Since that time, Melissa has focused on raising her three children and, in rare spare moments, on her writing. She currently resides in Texas with her family and her beloved menagerie of furry Muses.

www.ingramcontent.com/pod-product-compliance
Lightning Source LLC
Chambersburg PA
CBHW031418040426
42444CB00005B/634